Smell

First published in the U.S. in 1994 by Carolrhoda Books, Inc.
c/o The Lerner Group
241 First Avenue North, Minneapolis, Minnesota 55401

Copyright © 1993 Wayland (Publishers) Ltd., Hove, East Sussex
First published 1993 Wayland (Publishers) Ltd.

Library of Congress Cataloging-in-Publication Data

Suhr, Mandy.
    Smell / written by Mandy Suhr ; illustrated by Mike Gordon.
        p.   cm. – (I'm alive)
    Originally published: Wayland Publishers, 1993.
    ISBN 0-87614-835-6
    1. Smell–Juvenile literature. [1. Smell. 2. Senses and
sensation.] I. Gordon, Mike, ill. II. Title. III. Series: Suhr, Mandy.
I'm alive.
QP458.S84 1994   93-44189
612.8'6–dc20   CIP
                                                                    AC

Printed in Italy by Rotolito Lombarda S.p.A., Milan
Bound in the United States of America

1 2 3 4 5 6 – P/OS – 99 98 97 96 95 94

Smell

written by Mandy Suhr
illustrated by Mike Gordon

Carolrhoda Books, Inc.
Minneapolis

Close your eyes and sniff the air.
What can you smell?

5

There are thousands of different
kinds of smells.

Some smells are sweet...

and some smells are stale.

Some things are nice to smell...

but some are not so nice!

Some smells can make you
feel hungry.

But sometimes, being able to smell
is not such a good thing!

Smells are made of tiny particles.
They float in the air and are so small
that you can't see them.

13

When you breathe, these tiny
particles go into your nose.

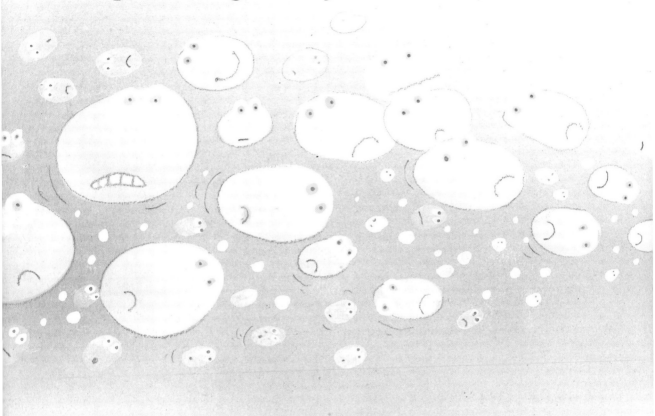

They cling to the sticky mucus that
is inside your nose.

smell detectors

Under the mucus are special smell detectors. They collect the particles.

15

The particles stick to the smell
detectors, which send messages to
your brain. These messages help
your brain to figure out what kind
of smell you are smelling.

All your senses work together, but smell and taste are special partners.

When you smell something, it helps you to figure out what the taste will be like.

When you have a cold, you can't smell very well.

This is because your nose is blocked.
Often you can't tell what things taste
like either.

Some animals are really good at
smelling. Dogs can find things just
by smelling the scent that is left
behind where something or someone
has been. This is why dogs are often
used to help find missing people.

23

Being able to smell
can sometimes warn
you of danger.

24

Often you can smell things you might not be able to see, like gas or something burning.

What is your favorite smell?

26

Play this game at school or at home with a friend. Can you guess what something is just by smelling it?

A note to adults

"I'm Alive" is a series of books designed especially for preschoolers and beginning readers. These books look at how the human body works and develops. They compare the human body to plants, animals, and objects that are already familiar to children.

Here are some activities that use what kids already know to learn more about their sense of smell.

Activities

1. Make a poster of smells. Take a sheet of construction paper and draw a line down the middle. Label one side "good smells" and the other side "bad smells." Then look through old magazines for pictures of things that smell good or bad to you, such as fresh-baked bread or garbage. Cut out the pictures and paste them on the construction paper. If you do this activity as a group, be sure to take a look at other people's choices. You may find that something that smells great to you smells terrible to someone else!

2. Take a walk in the city. How many things can you smell? Car exhaust? Food from a restaurant? Flowers in a window box? Notice both good smells and bad smells. Then take a walk in the country (a park will do). What do you smell? Fresh-cut grass? Flowers in a garden? A fishy pond? How are city and country smells different? How are they the same?

3. Here's a game you can play with your nose. Spray a handkerchief heavily with cologne. Leave the room while someone hides the handkerchief. Then see how long it takes you to find the handkerchief, using your nose to sniff it out.

4. The next time you smell food cooking in the kitchen, don't ask, "What's for dinner?" Instead try to figure it out with your nose. Is that roast beef cooking? Or maybe it's chicken. And what's that wonderful smell coming from the oven? Could it be apple pie?

Titles in This Series

How I Breathe

I Am Growing

I Can Move

When I Eat

Sight

Touch

Smell

Taste

Hearing

DATE DUE